PARROTS

Written and edited by **Lucy Baker**

Consultant Ian Dawson, Librarian,
Royal Society for the Protection of Birds

TWO-CAN

First published in Great Britain in 1991 by
Two-Can Publishing Ltd
27 Cowper Street
London EC2A 4AP

© Two-Can Publishing Ltd, 1991

© Text by Lucy Baker, 1991
Typesetting by The Creative Text Partnership
Printed in Italy by Amadeus – Rome

All rights reserved. No part of this publication may be reproduced,
stored in a retrieval system, or transmitted in any form or by any
means, electronic, mechanical, photocopying, recording or otherwise,
without prior written permission of the copyright owner.
The JUMP! logo and the word JUMP! are registered trade marks.

British Library Cataloguing in Publication Data
Baker, Lucy
Parrots.
1. Parrots
I. Title
598.71

ISBN 1-85434-092-1

Photographic Credits:
Front Cover NHPA p.4 ZEFA p.5 Gerard Lacz/NHPA p.6 Steve Littlewood/Oxford Scientific Films p.7 (left) Alain Compost/Bruce Coleman Ltd. (right) K W Fink/Ardea p.8-9 Gunter Zeisler/Bruce Coleman Ltd. p.10 Jean-Paul Ferrero/Ardea p.11 Partridge Films Ltd./Oxford Scientific Films p.12 K W Fink/ZEFA p.13 Konrad Wothe/Bruce Coleman Ltd. p.14 Frank Schneidermeyer/Oxford Scientific Films p.15 Harolds Palo Jnr./NHPA p.16 Jane Burton/Bruce Coleman Ltd. p.17 Jean-Paul Ferrero/Ardea p.18 K W Fink/Ardea p.19 Graeme Chapman/Ardea

Illustration Credits:
Back Cover p.4-19 David Cook/Linden Artists p.20-21 Steve Ling/Linden Artists p.22-23 Claire Legemah p.24-25 Ken Hooks/Jeremy Clegg p.26-30 John Rignall/Linden Artists p.31 Alan Rogers

CONTENTS

Looking at parrots	4
Parrot families	6
Parrot life	8
Feeding time	10
Courtship	12
In the nest hole	14
Pet parrots	16
Parrot problems	18
Forest game	20
Parrot mask	22
Find the parrots	24
A new paradise	26
True or false?	31
Index	32

LOOKING AT PARROTS

Parrots are one of the most popular and easily recognised bird groups. They are usually thick-bodied, short-legged birds with colourful feathers.

All parrots have hooked bills like those of hawks and eagles. The parrot's bill can be opened very wide and closed again with great force.

Parrots can be found in tropical countries all round the world and in one or two southern regions like New Zealand. They are most common in South America and Australia.

Parrots live in lush rainforests, dense jungles and open countryside and spend most of their time in the tops of the trees.

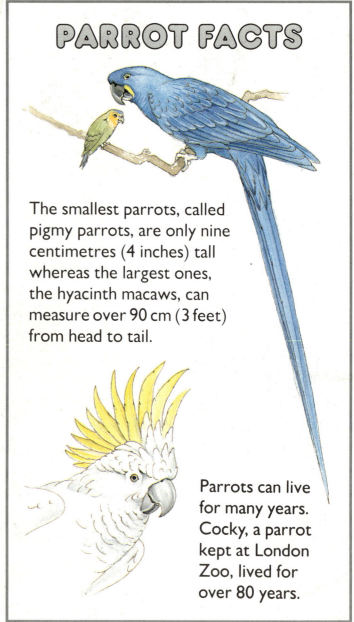

PARROT FACTS

The smallest parrots, called pigmy parrots, are only nine centimetres (4 inches) tall whereas the largest ones, the hyacinth macaws, can measure over 90 cm (3 feet) from head to tail.

Parrots can live for many years. Cocky, a parrot kept at London Zoo, lived for over 80 years.

▶ Parrots have four claws on each foot — two facing forwards and two facing backwards. This allows them to get a strong grip on branches but often makes them awkward on flat ground. The parrot in this picture is called a Levaillant's amazon.

◀ These two red and yellow macaws are climbing a tree. Most parrots prefer to climb trees rather than fly from branch to branch. Can you see how one of the macaws is using its bill like an extra leg?

FEEDING TIME

Nuts and seeds form the basic diet of most parrots but soft fruits, plants and insects may be eaten. The lories and lorikeets extract the sweet pollen and nectar from the inside of flowers with their special brush-tipped tongues.

Farmers consider some parrots pests because they raid fields of grain and fruit orchards. The parrots swoop down in great flocks and eat up the farmer's produce.

Parrots often hold their food with one foot while they are eating. They use their powerful bills to crack open hard nutshells and their long, tubular tongues to remove kernels from inside. Even the largest parrots can get the tiniest seeds out of sprays of millet because all parrots have a very sensitive tongue.

Parrots swallow their food without chewing it. They store it in a special pouch inside their throat called a crop and digest it when they are hungry. Food stored in the parrot's crop may be regurgitated and fed to young chicks or to the parrot's partner during the mating season.

▶ The white-fronted parrot in this picture is using its claws to hold a small berry.
▼ Rainbow lorikeets live in large flocks in Eastern Australia. As well as taking the nectar from flowers, these friendly birds will also feed from the hands of strangers.

FEEDING FACTS

Parrots have to eat grit and small pebbles to help them digest their food properly.

The largest parrots can crack open brazil nuts with their powerful bills.

COURTSHIP

Large species of parrot usually start breeding when they are three to four years old, but smaller parrots start mating much earlier — when they are one or two years old.

Mating takes place during the spring months or after the rainy season when food is most plentiful. Male parrots perform courtship displays to attract their partners. They may bow

▲ The yellow-headed parrot, above, is probably collecting material for its nesting hole. Some parrots line their nesting hole with leaves or sticks, but often the only thing in the hollow is a layer of wood chippings.

◀ Mating parrots are very loving to one another. They help clean each other's feathers and they feed each other food. These two birds grooming each other are hyacinth macaws.

their heads, wag their tail feathers, stamp their feet or flap their wings as part of their display. Once a partnership has been established, parrot couples often remain together for life.

Although most parrots do not build nests, they still have to find a place to lay their eggs and raise their young. Most parrots lay their eggs in the hollows found in tree trunks and branches. Both birds clean out the hollow and they may chip away some wood. They need to make it big enough for their growing chicks.

NESTING FACTS

Unlike most parrots, monk parrots build nests. The enormous structures house up to 20 families and are so strong that other birds may live on the roof.

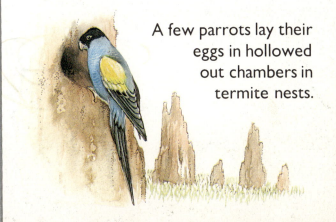

A few parrots lay their eggs in hollowed out chambers in termite nests.

IN THE NEST HOLE

Although some female parrots may lay up to eight eggs, two to five is more usual. The eggs are laid at the bottom of the nesting hole and one of the parrots usually sits on them until they hatch. The eggs must be kept warm or the developing chicks may die. It is usually the female who keeps the eggs warm, while the male finds food.

Parrots' eggs take from two and a half to five weeks to hatch. The young chicks crack open their shells using a special egg tooth that grows on the top of their bills. The egg tooth drops off once the tiny bird has hatched.

Parrot chicks are born blind and helpless. Their mother usually looks after them for the first few days. She feeds them food brought to her by their father. Then, both birds share their parental tasks.

◀ A sun conure calls from its nesting hole.
▼ A bird's eye view of a blue macaw's nesting hole reveals three eggs buried among the wood chippings.

PARROT CHICKS

Parrot chicks have no feathers when they first hatch. They are naked, blind and helpless.

Their tiny bodies become covered in soft down and then stronger feathers grow that give the birds their shape and enable them to fly.

Both parents feed their chicks while they learn to fly and find food. Some chicks remain with their family or their family's flock. Others leave their parents to join another parrot flock.

PET PARROTS

Wild parrots are noisy birds, known for their loud, piercing shrieks and squawks. However, captive parrots have a remarkable talent for mimicry. They can learn to say many different words and phrases. For this reason, and because they are such colourful birds, parrots have been popular pets for centuries.

In Roman times, parrots were kept in ornate cages and taught to praise the emperor of the time. For a while they became so common that they were cooked and served as a delicacy.

Parrots are also very friendly birds. Some wild parrots will perch on a person's shoulder or feed from his or her hand. Captive parrots like a lot of attention and hate to be left alone during the day.

The best talking parrots are thought to be African greys and amazons, but other parrots can learn to talk too. Parrots do not just learn to mimic words. They can also learn to sniff or cough and repeat the noise of a telephone ringing or a dog barking.

▶ African grey parrots have a reputation as the best talkers of the parrot family.

▼ The budgerigar's proper name is the Australian shell parakeet. It is one of the most common parrots to be kept as a pet.

PET FACTS

Pet parrots love to have their heads scratched by their owners.

Parrots are intelligent birds. They quickly master simple games or puzzles.

Lovebirds like to bathe in a saucer of water.

PARROT PROBLEMS

▲ A group of long-billed corellas play on telephone wires to pass the hours.

Every year millions of birds are taken from their wild homes. The way in which the birds are caught and transported is often very cruel.

To lure wild parrots into their nets, some parrot traders use decoys — captive parrots whose distress calls bring wild flocks to the ground. Other traders cover the parrots' night-time roosts with glue. When the birds land, they have little chance of escape. Eggs and parrot chicks may be stolen from the parrots' nesting holes.

Captured parrots have to be taken many miles by road, sea and air to be sold. During the journey, they may be crammed into small crates or squeezed into plastic tubes. Often, they are not given food or water until they arrive at the marketplace. For every ten parrots caught as many as eight may die because of cruel transportation methods.

There is little effective control of the bird trade. Certain parrots and other exotic birds are being hunted to extinction. The more rare a bird becomes, the more money it is worth.

It is not only the bird trade that poses a threat to the world's parrots. In many places, their homes are being destroyed too. Most parrots live in wooded areas. Some even rely on one particular type of tree. Many of the most colourful parrots live in rainforests that are being rapidly destroyed. Some scientists believe the world's rainforests will have disappeared in less than 100 years.

Conservation groups and bird societies all over the world protest about the cruel methods used by the bird trade. They are fighting to keep certain natural habitats unchanged so that parrots and other woodland animals can survive. Thanks to the work of such groups, many countries have banned the import of wild parrots. However, the Spix's macaw and some other parrots have already been hunted to extinction and are only found in zoos.

▼ These young blue rumped parrotlets must live in dark, cramped conditions until their captor finds a buyer.

SAVE THE PARROT

If you want to help parrots and other wild birds, there are lots of wildlife charities, bird societies and conservation groups to join. Your support will help them monitor the bird trade and save natural habitats.

If you buy a parrot, make sure it was bred in captivity and not taken from its natural home.

PARROT MASK

There are lots of ways to decorate masks. Here are a few things to try.

fabric
paint
crayons
coloured paper

▶ Our mask was made by cutting this basic shape from cardboard and decorating it with paper.

Try making a mask. It's easy to do and fun to wear. All you need is a piece of cardboard, a length of elastic or string and a pair of scissors.

Draw a basic mask shape on to the card. Remember to make two holes for your eyes and a small hole at each side of the mask.

Carefully cut out your mask and then decide how you are going to decorate it. Try some of the ideas in the picture on the left. When your mask is decorated, thread the elastic or string through the two holes at the sides of the mask. Now your mask is ready to wear!

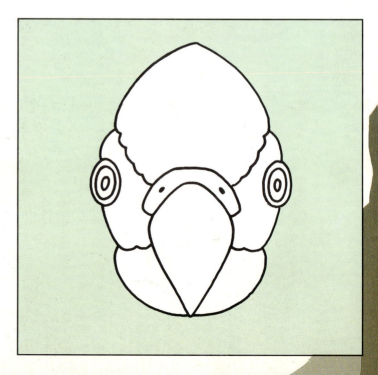

A NEW PARADISE

BY LUCY BAKER

Suki and Samson were scarlet macaws — huge birds with brilliant red, yellow and blue feathers and very long pointed tails. You can see birds like them in pet shops all round the world but Suki and Samson were wild birds from Central America.

Suki and Samson were sad. Their home — the beautiful rainforest — seemed empty and quiet. They were sitting close to each other, high in the branches of an exotic tree. They felt as though everything had changed.

The chattering monkeys were still there, fooling around in the upper branches. A sloth was still making its slow, deliberate way through the neighbouring tree. In fact, only one thing had changed — Suki and Samson's chicks were missing.

The two macaws had just popped out to feed on a nearby tree and when they came back their two young chicks had disappeared. Three times they had tried to raise a family, and three times the young, vulnerable birds had disappeared.

They knew what had happened. Their parents had warned them. There were bad men that roamed the forest looking for animals. They did not want to kill and eat the animals, like big cats and fearsome eagles do. They wanted to put the animals in cages and take them away.

This time two men had arrived to capture Suki and Samson's chicks. One had climbed up to the nesting

hole with speed and skill, while the other stood below.

The monkeys had howled and screeched from a distance, but the sloth had watched quietly, not daring to move. He had thought to himself, if they see me, they will take me too.

Everyone had seen the two bleating chicks as they were lifted out of their nesting hole. The tiny birds caught one quick glimpse of their wondrous home and then disappeared. The bad men had put them into a small wicker basket, closed the lid, and gone.

Samson and Suki made up their minds. They must go away. How could they ever raise a family while those men roamed their forest floor? They would find another place to live, a new paradise.

The very next morning, at the crack of dawn, they left their homely roost with a loud squawking cry. They announced their plans to the monkeys, the sloth and all the other animals they loved. Bursting through the forest canopy, they began their long flight.

Samson and Suki stayed close together, their wings almost touching. At least they had each other. And this was an adventure. Never before had they travelled outside the forest.

Their first day of flying passed peacefully. It was very tiring but Suki and Samson followed the course of a river and stopped regularly to eat and drink. As the sun went down, they found a beautiful blossoming tree at the edge of the river and slept there through the night.

The second day went well too. But on the third day Suki and Samson had a terrible shock. The forest had disappeared. There were fiercesome fires raging and noisy machinery cutting down trees. The further they went the worse it became.

That night they had to really search for a tree to sleep in. Suki was worried and would not settle. What if there was no more forest? What if they could not find food? How long would their journey take?

Samson was worried too but he fed Suki some of his stored food and preened her feathers. "We are going to find a new home soon. You must be patient and strong," he said.

By the fifth day, things looked bad. They had been travelling for three days over scarred land. The rivers were poisoned and the trees were burnt or sliced. They were hungry and tired and there was no forest in sight.

Still Samson calmed and comforted Suki. "We will find our new home soon, you wait and see."

On the sixth day they caught sight of a green horizon. They had passed dusty towns and blackened forests, baked grounds and regimental grass fields. Now, at last, the forest was back.

On the seventh morning, they reached their new home. Samson flew ahead of Suki and then back to her side. The further into the forest they travelled, the more they liked what they saw. There were no fires, no buildings, no loud machinery.

Best of all, there were other macaws. Large, loud flocks of colourful birds filled the sky. The birds greeted each other and Suki and Samson told their story.

Hundreds of birds gathered round to hear what they had to say. Suki and Samson told them why they had left their own forest and what they had seen on the way.

Some of the older birds nodded their heads wisely as Samson spoke. Others looked sad and troubled, as if they had been reminded of something bad. The younger ones looked at one another, uncertain and mystified.

After Samson had finished his tale a large green macaw explained. "You have come to the right place. The men here are not bad. They do not have guns or cages. Some have strange black boxes that make a clicking noise, but most of them only carry a pencil and pad."

"The only bad thing our men have done," added another bird, "is build a huge, unfriendly fence. It stretches for miles and miles."

Samson and Suki thought about this and then Suki corrected him. "Your fence is not a bad thing. It is not to keep the animals in — it is to keep the bad men out." And all the birds agreed.

TRUE OR FALSE?

Which of these facts are true and which ones are false? If you have read this book carefully you will know the answers.

1. All parrots have hooked bills.
2. Parrots have five claws on each foot.
3. Most parrots have a long, thin tongue.

4. Lorikeets eat nectar and pollen from flowers.
5. Cockatoos and cockatiels are the only parrots that have head crests.
6. Parrots are quiet birds that like to live alone.
7. Parrots sleep in large, twig nests.

8. Parrots eat grit and small pebbles to help with their digestion.
9. The parrot's crop is inside its stomach.
10. Most parrots lay their eggs in termite nests.
11. Parrot chicks are born with all their feathers.
12. Parrots can learn to copy voices and other sounds.

13. Pet parrots love to have their heads scratched.
14. Parrots use their beaks as an extra limb when climbing in the treetops.
15. Most parrots fly at night.

Answers: 1. True; 2. False; 3. False; 4. True; 5. False; 6. True; 7. False; 8. True; 9. False; 10. False; 11. False; 12. True; 13. True; 14. True; 15. False.

INDEX

African grey parrot 16,17
age 4
amazon 4,5,6,16
Australian shell parakeet 16

bathing 17
bills 4,9,10
bird societies 19
blue rumped parrotlet 19
budgerigar 16

calls 16
captive parrots 16,18
chicks 10,15,18
cockatiel 7
cockatoo 7
conservation groups 19
crests 7
crop 10

diet 10

egg tooth 15
eggs 13,15,18

feathers 4,7,17
feeding 8,10
flight 8
flocks 8,15

green macaw 8

habitats 4
hanging parrot 6
hyacinth macaw 4,12
hybrid macaw 7

Levaillant's amazon 4,5
long-billed corella 18
lories 6,10
lorikeets 6,10
lovebirds 6,7

macaws 4,7,8,12
mating 12
mimicry 16

nests 13
nesting holes 13,14,15,18

owl parrot 6

parents 15
pests 10
pets 16,17
pigmy parrot 4
problems 18,19

rainbow lorikeet 10
red and yellow macaw 4

scarlet macaw 8
size 4
sleep 8
sulphur-crested cockatoo 4,7
sun conure 14

tongues 6
traders 18

white-fronted parrot 11

yellow-headed parrot 13